RECLAIMING THE SUFFICIENCY OF SCRIPTURE

ROB RIENOW

randall house
114 Bush Rd I Nashville, TN 37217 I randallhouse.com

ISBN 9780892656752

Printed in the United States of America

Dedicated to my mother, Angie, who taught me to love and believe the Bible.

TABLE OF CONTENTS

INTRODUCTION

The purpose of this book is to start a conversation about the most important thing in the world—the advance of the glory and Gospel of Jesus Christ to the ends of the earth. Before Jesus ascended to the Father, He gave His followers this mission,

> "Go therefore and make disciples of all nations, baptizing them in the name of the Father and of the Son and of the Holy Spirit, teaching them to observe all that I have commanded you. And behold, I am with you always, to the end of the age."
> —Matthew 28:19-20

Most likely, you are a part of a local church that speaks often of this Great Commission. Your church probably even has a mission statement that draws much of its focus from these words of Jesus.

With mission statement in hand (or at least in the desk drawer) we pack the calendar with innovative programs, stretch the budget, work overtime to recruit volunteers, neglect our families for days or weeks at a time, and then...

Can we honestly say that our jam-packed church calendar and our dynamic programs for every demographic group are making mature disciples for Jesus Christ?

When was the last time you looked at your church's results? Are the Christians in your church growing in faith, godliness, and character? Are the Christians in your church deepening in their love for, understanding of, and obedience to the Bible? Are the Christians in your church becoming better equipped and more dedicated to evangelism and service in their communities and beyond?

The reality is some Christian churches today are offering more and more programming, and making fewer and fewer true disciples. Just because the seats are full, does not mean disciples are being made.

What I was missing

During my first eighteen years of pastoral ministry, I was blessed to serve as the Youth and Family Pastor at Wheaton Bible Church in the Chicago suburbs. I am grateful for these many years in a special church, the great friends I served with, and the transforming lessons God taught me.

As I will share with you in the pages ahead, God dramatically changed my family and my pastoral ministry in 2004. I was a leader at church, but not at home. I was discipling other people's children, but not mine. Through that journey, God opened my eyes to the spiritual power of the Christian family! Since that time, I have sought to do all I can to accelerate Christian families for Gospel living, and to help churches to equip families for this mission.

However, the summer in 2004 was not the first time I had heard God's call to parents to disciple their children. As a youth pastor, I read various books and articles about how the modern youth ministry model had replaced parents, and that we needed to return to the biblical model of home-centered discipleship. While I agreed with some of the critique against the modern youth ministry model I was leading, to be candid, I thought many of these pastors, writers, and speakers were a little extreme. I thought they were over-reacting, being unnecessarily negative about what churches were doing to reach the next generation, and were wrongly placing too much emphasis on parents and the family.

I now look back at some of those books and articles, which I thought were "extreme," and now have great appreciation for them.

So what changed? Why did I reject a vision for family ministry ten years ago, but fully embrace it today? What was I missing?

The post-conference disconnect

In recent years, I have been on the other side of the conversation. I am now the one pleading with pastors to embrace a vision and strategy for ministry that engages the Christian family. Here is a predictable series of events:

A church leader attends a family ministry conference such as D6[1] or AMFM[2]. A speaker stands up and begins the message with two broad points.

> Point 1: It is not the job of the local church to disciple children; it is the job of parents.

> Point 2: Look at God's call to parents in Deuteronomy 6, Psalm 78, and Ephesians 6.

The message then moves into application of these principles for families and churches. So far, so good. Over the course of the conference, God gives the church leader a passion and vision for "family ministry." He returns home. In the staff meeting the week after the conference, he shares what he learned, and his burden and sense of calling for the church to move in the direction of family ministry.

Where does this conversation lead? Usually, there are warm and supportive thoughts expressed from the rest of the staff. A general encouragement is given to the leader who attended the conference to keep thinking about how the church can "better support families." But the vision, passion, and urgency for paradigm change is not shared. Why? Something is missing.

The sufficiency of Scripture

I now know why I could not hear the message of family discipleship ten years ago. Despite seminary degrees, I was not grounded in the doctrine of the sufficiency of Scripture.

Consider again the two big "points" from the message at the family ministry conference. These might sound simple. "It is not the job of the local church to disciple their children; it is the job of parents. Now, look at what God says about this in Deuteronomy 6, etc."

These are not simple statements. In fact, they are dramatic doctrinal proclamations. The first point, "it is not the job of the church but the family," is a statement of jurisdictional theology. My generation has little or no jurisdictional theology. We don't think of the specific roles and responsibilities God has given in pages of Scripture to individuals, families, churches, and governments. One urgent example of this is how many in my generation seem not to care if the government takes care of our parents in their old age.

But it is the foundation under the second point that makes all the difference. This was the missing piece for me! When we say, "God called parents in the Bible to be the primary disciplers of their children, therefore parents today should be the primary disciplers of their children," we are using the Bible as a final authority for ministry methodology. We are not only claiming the Bible is sufficient for doctrine (God loves children) and for the will of God (God wants children evangelized and discipled)–but also for how God wants His will carried out and who should do it.

Because I did not understand or embrace the doctrine of the sufficiency of Scripture for every matter of faith and practice, I rejected the message of family discipleship.

Advancing the Gospel

This is not a book about family ministry. It is about powering and directing every ministry of the Christian family and the local church with Scripture.

My writings will begin, proceed, and end with the conviction that God, in the Bible, has told us not only what He wants done, but also how He wants it done. God has given us both the ends, and the means of ministry...His mission and His methods. I am convinced that the doctrine of the sufficiency of Scripture is the lost key we need to accelerate the Great Commission!

I have prayed about many things during the preparation of this book. I have prayed God's words, not mine, would take center stage. I have prayed, according to Psalm 138:2, that the Lord would "exalt above all things, His name and His Word." Thanks again for joining me in this journey.

God's Love,

Rob Rienow

ENDNOTES

[1]www.d6conference.com

[2]www.amfmonline.com

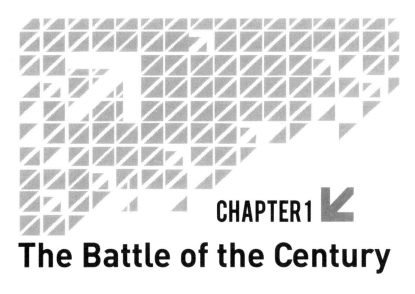

CHAPTER 1

The Battle of the Century

"…For you have exalted above all things your name and your word."

—Psalm 138:2b

The church service finished about fifteen minutes ago. You are talking with a group of Christian friends, when a visitor approaches you and says, "I have some questions. Can you talk to me?"

You and your friends are eager to help. "Sure, what's on your mind?"

"Well, for starters, I have been thinking a lot about Heaven. What will it be like there?"

What would you say? My guess is you would begin to talk about how God will one day create a brand new earth, and that those who have trusted Christ will live together with Him. In Heaven, there will be no more tears, or crying or pain! It will be a perfect place, free from all sin and evil, and it will last forever.

The visitor responds softly, "Heaven sure sounds like a wonderful place. I don't have much hope in this life…but I could hope for that. How do you know these things?"

"These aren't my ideas. In the Bible, God has given us the truth about Heaven, Hell, and His plan to save us from our sins. The things I am telling you are written down at the end of the book of Revelation."

Now imagine that one of your friends eagerly chimes into the conversation and said, "You are right, Heaven is going to be wonderful! Just last week, I was watching this amazing show on TV, and a man was being interviewed who actually had gone to Heaven. Then this person was brought back to life. He said after he died, the first thing that happened is he was invited to a banquet table where he had a meal with all of his relatives who had died. After that, he was teleported to the pearly gates where Moses and Noah were standing. They told him he had not been good enough in this life to enter Heaven, so he was being sent back to try and be a better person. It was very inspiring and made me want to be a better person too. He wrote a great book about his experience, you should really check it out."

The conversation has taken a new direction. How are you feeling right now? I hope you are about ready to jump out of your skin and are formulating a plan to interrupt your friend as quickly as possible!

But what's the problem? Why would you be concerned about this shift in the conversation? The answer is obvious. When someone asks us a question such as, "What is Heaven like?" we only need to make reference to one book—the Bible.

The Bible is sufficient to answer this question. Only in the Bible do we have God's revealed truth about what Heaven will be like. To bring any other source of knowledge to the conversation is at best dangerous, and at worst heresy.

When it comes to questions such as,

- "Why did Jesus have to die?"
- "How can I be saved?"
- "Why should I be baptized?"
- "Who is the Holy Spirit?"
- "Where is God?"

Most Christians I know would use their Bible, and their Bible alone, to find the answers. They might need to make use of a reference book, but only so they might find the appropriate Scriptures. Christians believe that not only is the Bible true, it is enough. It is sufficient.

But what about these questions:

- "What should be our strategy in youth ministry?"
- "What should we teach this year in women's ministry?"
- "Should we have children in our worship services?"
- "How can we reach more singles?"
- "How can we do a better job caring for the poor?"

For many years in pastoral ministry, I rarely opened my Bible to seek answers to these questions. Think of your own first response to questions like these. If someone asked you, "What should be our strategy in youth ministry?" Would you begin your reply with, "Well, in the Bible, God speaks to this issue and He lays out for us His plan for how children are to be evangelized and discipled. Let me show you…"?

Or what about, "How can we reach more singles?" Would your first response be, "That is a great question! God has a lot to say about singleness in the Bible, and in the New Testament we find some very specific things that the early church did to minister to singles. Let me show you…"?

This next statement may shock you. In some seminaries today, pastors are not trained to use the Bible for ministry decisions. We are trained to use the Bible for "doctrinal" issues like the ones listed above, but when it comes to daily church decisions pragmatism, innovation, creativity, and human wisdom rule the day.

For the first decade of my pastoral ministry, I sought to get all my "doctrine" from the Bible, while I made ministry decisions myself and with my staff team. The Bible was enough for me when it came to my systematic theology, but not enough when it came to how God's institutions of the family and the local church should function.

The battle is on

The church faced a cataclysmic battle in the 20th century. A war was waged over the Bible. Was it true? Could it be trusted? Was it inspired and authoritative? Many churches and denominations were lost, as they abandoned their belief in the Bible as the inspired Word of God.[1]

However, God never abandons His church. In the lives of millions of Christians, thousands of churches, and many denominations, the Holy Spirit defeated the demonic attack of liberalism, and there was a renewed commitment to the authority and truth of the Bible. The so-called Search for the Historical Jesus was demonstrated to be fraught with inconsistencies and poor scholarship.[2] Significant archaeological finds dramatically increased in the 20th century, and to the shock and amazement of the world, continued to support the true history as recorded in the Bible.[3]

The secular media loves to ridicule Christians any chance they get. Don't you think if there were an archaeological find that conclusively contradicted the history in the Bible that it would be on the front page of every paper? It would be common knowledge and trotted out in every spiritual conversation, "You know, the find they made over in Egypt totally disproves what the Bible says." Certainly, attempts are made toward this end, but the "evidence" eventually proves flimsy. Archaeology consistently proves and supports the history of the Bible.

My guess is that if you were to ask your congregation, "How many of you believe the Bible is completely true and trustworthy?" almost every hand would go up! Praise God!

I can remember reading both the scholarly and popular writings defending God's Word against any and all comers. In high school, I devoured Josh McDowell's, Evidence That Demands a Verdict[4], and More Than a Carpenter.[5] My son is now starting to read them. In college and graduate school, it was a privilege to be able learn from the more rigorous and technical apologetic resources dealing with hermeneutics and canonical development.[6] You do not need to check your brain at the door to follow Christ and believe the Bible.[7]

At this point, I need to make a dangerous assumption about you. I am going to assume that you are completely convinced the Bible is the inspired, true, authoritative Word of God. Everything that follows in this book is based on that core conviction.

If you are not convinced and convicted about the inspiration and truth of the Bible, you may want to stop reading and take a look at some of the books I mentioned above. If you don't already believe the Bible is true, the rest of this book will make little sense.

The Bible is true but is it enough?

The church faces a new battle in the 21st century. The battle in many Christian churches today is not, "Is the Bible true?" but, "Is the Bible enough?" The challenge in the 20th century was over inerrancy, the challenge in the 21st century is over sufficiency.

Do we believe the Bible, or do we believe the Bible alone? Do we allow the Bible to shape our thoughts and opinions on every subject? How we answer these questions radically shapes how we live out our faith, and seek to advance the Gospel of our supreme Lord and Savior, Jesus Christ.

In some ways, the issue at the heart of the Protestant Reformation has returned. During the 14th-16th centuries the church powerfully united, and powerfully divided around five "onlys." In Latin, we call them the five "solas."

Only is a powerful word. It is extreme. It picks a fight. It draws a line in the sand.

During the Reformation, believers in Jesus Christ staked their families, their fortunes, their reputations, and their very lives on five *solas*...five onlys. These are words many died for, and many are still[8] dying for.

Sola Scriptura – Only Scripture—The Bible and the Bible alone is our authority in all matters of faith and life.[9]

Sola Gratia – Only Grace—We don't deserve salvation and forgiveness. We are saved by the unearned loving grace of God.[10]

Sola Fide – Only Faith—We do not earn points with God through doing good things. We cannot earn His favor or salvation by being virtuous. We cannot lose salvation by being extra bad. We are forgiven and made right when we respond to God's grace with repentance and faith.[11]

Solus Christus – Only Christ—God has made one and only one way for sinful men and women to be forgiven and saved, and that is through Jesus' death, resurrection, and glorious ascension.[12]

Soli Deo Gloria – Only for the Glory of God—This is the purpose of life—the purpose of working, eating, marrying, coming to church, planting your garden, reading your Bible, and volunteering—it is all for the glory of God.[13]

It was on these five biblical doctrines that men like John Wycliffe, Jan Hus, William Tyndale, Martin Luther, and John Calvin sought to bring about a re-formation of the church. *Sola Scriptura* served as the foundation for the other four *solas*. What would you use to teach someone the doctrine of grace? How would you seek to persuade someone that Jesus was the Christ, the one and only Son of God? What would you use to explain to someone the nature of God, and what it means to worship Him? You would use the Bible, and the Bible alone, to teach and understand the doctrines of grace, faith, Christ, and worship. The protestant reformation was centered on, grounded in, and built upon the doctrine of the sufficiency of the Bible.

The history of Christianity in general, and the history of each Christian person specifically, is a constant journey of reforming and recalibrating. Satan and the world are constantly seeking to pull the church and individual believers away from the true worship of God. This has been so true in my life. I go through times when I give the enemy a foothold, allow a sin to grow in a dark corner, or I find myself thinking just like the world. God then brings the truth of the Bible to that situation, the Holy Spirit convicts my heart, I repent, confess, and by God's grace get back on track. God continually forms me, and re-forms me into the image of His Son. Most nights during family worship, as my children would tell you, I thank God for His grace, mercy, and patience with me, a sinner.

The same is true in the history of the church. Individual churches and entire denominations at times have fallen into disobedience, false teaching, and heresy. There are numerous instructions in the New Testament that elders/pastors are to make absolutely sure they guard the doctrine taught in the church. Make sure everything comes from the Bible! Don't have any wiggle room for false teachers who want to bring in legalism, who want to bring in ideas from the godless culture around us, or who want to mix faith in Christ with other world religions.

Tragically, this is exactly what happens in personal lives, in churches, and entire global networks of churches. If you don't pull the weeds, they take over.

The Christian life is one of continually re-forming, always seeking to re-align our churches, our families, and ourselves with the true worship of God, as He has revealed it to us in the pages of Scripture.

Believing the Bible is true is not enough

My goal is to explain how our belief in the sufficiency of Scripture is an essential foundation for the advance of the Gospel through our families and our churches.

There are many places in God's Word where He teaches us that the Bible is not only true, but sufficient. One of these texts is found in 2 Timothy 3:14-17. Paul writes this to Timothy, who was a young pastor:

"But as for you, continue in what you have learned and have firmly believed, knowing from whom you learned it and how from childhood you have been acquainted with the sacred writings, which are able to make you wise for salvation through faith in Christ Jesus. All Scripture is breathed out by God and profitable for teaching, for reproof, for correction, and for training in righteousness, that the man of God may be complete, equipped for every good work."[14]

Paul's first challenge to Timothy is for him to continue in what he has learned and has firmly believed. The more a believer studies God's book, the more one becomes intellectually convinced of its supernatural origin. Paul reminds Timothy that it was his mother and grandmother who first taught him God's Word. I can relate to Timothy in this. My mother became a Christian three months after I was born. My father was a secularist, and I praise God for a mother who filled my heart and mind with prayer and Scripture. As a side note here, parents, it is never too early to be reading the Bible to your children! Timothy's mom and grandma were reading Scripture to him "from infancy." My wife, Amy, has done this with our little ones as well. She puts the baby on a blanket, sets down some toys, and reads the Bible out loud. She calls it the "Bible spa," as the room is filled with the Words of God, and the Holy Spirit is working on a little heart.

God then, through Paul, teaches us truth about His Word.

> "...the sacred writings, which are able to make you wise for salvation through faith in Christ Jesus." —2 Timothy 3:15

The Bible has supernatural power. It is able to make us wise for salvation. The Bible has the ability through the Holy Spirit to bring us to repentance, transform us, change us, and renew our minds. God teaches us this in many places in His Word:

> "For the word of God is living and active, sharper than any two-edged sword, piercing to the division of soul and of spirit, of joints and of marrow, and discerning the thoughts and intentions of the heart." —Hebrews 4:12

The Bible is, in a spiritual sense, alive. The words of the Bible[15], because they are God's words, can penetrate the human heart, convict us of sin, and bring us face to face with the truth and love of God.

You have read from Hebrews 11:6 that, "without faith it is impossible to please [God]." But how do we get faith? If we need it to please Him, where does it come from?

> "So faith comes from hearing, and hearing through the word of Christ." —Romans 10:17

God's words are powerful. These revealed words, in the hands of the Holy Spirit, are able to bring people to repentance and faith in Jesus! When a sermon is preached, it is not the wise or eloquent words of the preacher that have the power to transform lives, rather it is when he speaks the words God has already given us. As a parent, my words do not have the power to renew the minds of my children, but God's words do!

If you were Satan and the demons, what do you think one of your strategies might be to keep people from faith in Christ, and for those who have faith, to keep them from growing? You would keep them as far away from the Bible as you possibly could. His attack in the church is subtle. Maybe he can get us to read a lot of Christian books, books about the Bible, but spend only a few minutes here and there in the real thing. In fact, the best use of your time right now might be to put this book down, and pick up His book. Most Christians I know, including myself, struggle to spend consistent time reading and studying the Bible. I believe it is because of this constant spiritual attack.

What is "the Word of God?"

The sufficiency of Scripture was the center of the conflict during the protestant reformation. At that time within the Roman Catholic Church, the Bible was only available in Latin and was administered only through the priests. It was thought and taught that the common people could not possibly be expected to read or understand the Bible on their own. This was not as much an issue of literacy, as it was theology. The Roman Catholic Church[16] at that time taught explicitly that the "Word of God" was not the

Bible alone, but rather the "Word of God" was the Bible along with the official interpretation of the church. This doctrine has continued to be taught and is expressed this way in the Catechism of the Catholic Church.[17]

> Both Scripture and Tradition must be accepted and honored with equal sentiments of devotion and reverence. (Catechism Part 1, 82)

> The task of giving an authentic interpretation of the Word of God has been entrusted to the living church alone. (Catechism Part 1, 85)

> The task of interpreting the Word of God authentically has been entrusted solely to the Pope and to the Bishops in communion with him...and this interpretation is irrevocably binding for the faith of Christian people. (Catechism Part 1, III, 94, and Part 1, III, 88)

The Roman Catholic Church believed 100% in the inerrancy, infallibility, and authority of the Bible. There was no debate in the church about whether or not the Bible was true, whether or not it was God's Word. The world-changing issue was whether or not the Bible was enough. Was the Bible sufficient?

The reformers were rightly convicted that the church of their day was teaching doctrines not found in Scripture. In addition, they saw the church instructing believers to worship God and practice their faith with means and methods also not found in Scripture.

Martin Luther risked his life for the doctrine of *sola Scriptura*. He believed that the Bible, and the Bible alone was the Word of God, and that no human being had authority over it, or beside it. Some of his most famous words were uttered on April 16, 1521 at the Diet of Worms when he proclaimed,

> "Unless I am convinced by Scripture and plain reason—I do not accept the authority of popes and councils, for they have

contradicted each other—my conscience is captive to the Word of God. I cannot and I will not recant anything, and to go against conscience is neither right nor safe. God help me. Amen."

When Luther translated the Bible into German and Guttenberg's moveable type enabled the Bible to be mass-produced, spiritual reformation spread like wildfire.

In the 1950 movie, Martin Luther, the writers pointedly and humorously portrayed a conversation between Luther and a fellow priest.

Priest: There is only one proper interpretation of Scripture, that which the church has established. What if Scripture were in the hands of the common man, for every potboy and swineherd to read in his own language and interpret for himself? What then?

Luther: Why, then we might have more Christians, Father!

Luther was an imperfect person like you and me, but he stood, and sometimes stood alone, on the foundation of *sola Scriptura*.

Take Your Stand

The church today is desperate for leaders who will take this same courageous stand! Not only do we believe the Bible, but we believe the Bible alone for every matter of faith and life. I am convinced we can trace much of the passivity and ineffectiveness in the modern church to our slippage on this vital doctrine.

It is surely a coincidence that the acronym for "Sufficiency of Scripture" is S.O.S., but as we dig deeper into this doctrine and its practical applications in our journey ahead, I hope you will join me in calling out "S.O.S!" to your brothers and sisters in Christ. The urgent call is not "Save Our Ship" but "Save Our Church!" As you will see, this is a battle we cannot afford to lose.

Questions for Reflection and Discussion:

1. Before reading this chapter, what would you have said was the difference between the doctrines of inerrancy and sufficiency?

2. To what degree does your church use the Bible as a sufficient guide for making ministry and programming decisions? How often is the Bible referred to when discussing ministry strategy?

3. What role does the Bible play in your personal life and in your family?

4. In what ways have you experienced spiritual attack aimed at keeping you away from the Bible?

ENDNOTES

[1] John Gresham Machen, *Christianity and Liberalism* (Charleston, SC: Bibliolife, 2009) – originally printed in 1923.

[2] Lee Strobel, *The Case for Christ* (Grand Rapids, MI: Zondervan, 1998).

[3] Alfred Hoerth and John McRay, *Bible Archaeology* (Grand Rapids, MI: Baker Books, 2006).

[4] Revised and Updated Edition – Josh McDowell, *The New Evidence That Demands a Verdict* (Nashville, TN: Thomas Nelson, 1999).

[5] Josh McDowell, *More Than a Carpenter* (Carol Stream, IL: Tyndale House Publishers, 2009).

[6] D. A. Carson and John D. Woodbridge, *Hermeneutics, Authority, and Canon* (Eugene, OR: Wipf and Stock Publishers, 2005).

[7] A great example of this principle can be found in Luke 1:4. Luke tells his readers that the essential purpose for his labors in writing down a careful history of what Jesus did and taught was so that we might have "certainty concerning the things [we] have been taught."

[8] See www.persecution.org.

[9] 2 Timothy 3:16-17.

[10]Ephesians 2:1-10.

[11]Ibid.

[12]John 14:6.

[13]1 Corinthians 10:31.

[14]Unless otherwise noted, Scripture references will be taken from the English Standard Version.

[15]I hold to the historical Christian doctrine that the Bible is inerrant and inspired in its original writing. This is not to say translations are of no value, but we should take great care to avoid preaching from translations which do not closely follow the original languages. God inspired the words (plenary inspiration) of the Bible, not just the ideas.

[16]In the early chapters of the book I will briefly summarize key biblical doctrines which stand in contrast to the historic teaching of the Roman Catholic Church. I have many close friends who are devout Catholics and we discuss these issues with respect, frankness, and love. All local churches and denominations are led by fallen and sinful men. No church or denomination is perfect. God only works through imperfect churches, because that is all there is. However, God used the men and the movement of the Reformation to millions, and now billions, back to the beliefs and practices of the early church, which are found in the Bible alone.

[17]*Catechism of the Catholic Church* (Mahwah, New Jersey: Paulist Press, 1994).

CHAPTER 2

Everything Important

> "Now the serpent was more crafty than any other beast of the field that the LORD God had made. He said to the woman, 'Did God actually say…'"
>
> —Genesis 3:1a

A few years ago, I had the honor of having lunch with Pastor Don Cole, from Moody Bible Institute. I asked him how he would define the doctrine of the sufficiency of Scripture. I'll never forget his words. "In the Bible, God has given us everything important, about everything important. He has given us everything that matters about everything that matters."

If something is important, God has given us everything we need to know about that issue in the Bible. If it matters, God speaks to it in the Bible, with absolute truth to all people, in all places, and in all times.

I am not saying the Bible is sufficient to learn everything about everything. You may need to learn how to do a root canal because you have chosen to be a dentist. You may need to learn how to repair a sink because you have chosen to be a plumber. While God has not given us all truth about all things[1], He has given us everything we need to know in order to faithfully serve Him and build His Kingdom.

Let's dig deeper by returning to our text in 2 Timothy 3, a keynote passage on the doctrine of sufficiency.

> "But as for you, continue in what you have learned and have firmly believed, knowing from whom you learned it and how from childhood you have been acquainted with the sacred writings, which are able to make you wise for salvation through faith in Christ Jesus. All Scripture is breathed out by God and profitable for teaching, for reproof, for correction, and for training in righteousness that the man of God may be complete, equipped for every good work." —2 Timothy 3:14-17

Zero in with me on verse 16. "All Scripture is breathed out by God and profitable for teaching, for reproof, for correction, and for training in righteousness…"

- Look at these four powerful words:
- Teaching—how to think right
- Reproof—how not to think wrong
- Correction—how not to act wrong
- Training in righteousness—how to act right

We could dive into each of these, but don't miss the intentional comprehensiveness. The Word of God speaks to both our thoughts and our actions. In the Bible, God tells us how to think correctly and He confronts wrong thinking. In the Bible, God tells us how to act correctly and He confronts wrong action. Can you see what God is claiming here? He is declaring, in no uncertain terms, that His Word speaks to every important matter of thought and life. All of life falls under one of those two categories.

The Slippery Slope

Consider these four questions. I have asked these same questions to Christian groups many times. I ask people, if their answer to the question is "yes," to raise their hands. Here we go:

Question 1: Do you believe the Bible is God's Word? In the context of a church service, or a Christian conference, almost every hand quickly shoots up.

Question 2: Do you believe the Bible is true in all that it intends to say?[2] Once again, the room is filled with bold hands in the air.

Question 3: Are you willing to submit all your thoughts and opinions on every subject to what it says? Awkward pause. A few hands are held high. About half the hands are partially raised.

Question 4: Are you willing to do what the Bible says, even if you don't want to? After a longer pause, about a quarter of the hands go up.

Do we, as Christians, believe the Bible is God's Word? Absolutely! No question about it. We believe the Bible comes from God. Do we believe it is true? Of course!

Are we willing to submit our thoughts and opinions on every subject to what it says? Whoa! Slow down there. Let's not get carried away.

In regard to the last question, "Are you willing to do what the Bible says, even if you don't want to?"—I am not talking about willful disobedience. There are plenty of times, to my shame, that I know well what God says about something in His Word, but I don't do it God's way, I do it my way. I sin. Maybe you have some experience with this as well. If there is anything "good" about willful disobedience, at least we acknowledge that God's Word is true and that we are choosing to disobey it.

I believe we have an increasing number of Christians today who say, "I know the Bible says to save sex for marriage, but the Bible was written a long time ago and I am not sure those standards apply in today's world." This person has made the decision that the Bible is not a sufficient guide for every matter of faith and practice, and replaced the clear teaching of God's Word with the values of the world. On the surface, this person has rejected God's plan for sex, but at a deeper level, they have rejected the authority of

His Word. Today we have a new kind of Christian, a person who says, "I love Jesus! But I don't believe every word of the Bible."

In the Beginning

Our response to the Word of God has been the central issue from the beginning of history. At the beginning of Genesis 3, God has already made Adam from the dust of the ground, and made Eve from Adam's rib. God's perfection is completely reflected in a perfect world. Then Satan, an angel who had rebelled against God and become a demon, comes to Eve. The first words out of his mouth set the stage for the same spiritual war that rages today.

> "Now the serpent was more crafty than any other beast of the field that the Lord God had made. He said to the woman, 'Did God actually say, 'You shall not eat from any tree in the garden?'" —Genesis 3:1

First words are important. They set the stage for what is to come. Satan leads with his primary strategy to lead people into sin, which is to make them doubt the words of God. Did God actually say? This is the first line of almost every demonic temptation. "Don't trust God's Word. God doesn't care about this. God hasn't spoken to this, and if He has, you don't need to listen to what He thinks. What do you think?" The central question facing the church today is whose authority, thoughts, words, and wisdom will we stand on?

How did Satan attack Jesus in the wilderness? He twisted and distorted the written Word that God had spoken through the prophets. How did Jesus defend Himself? He took up the sword of the Spirit, which is the Word of God. He would not allow the devil to twist and misuse even one word of the Bible. Jesus understood this was a battle for truth, who gets to define it, and whether or not he would live by it.

Jesus knew His Bible. Not only was He the divine author, but as a man He carefully studied it. The doctrine of the sufficiency of Scripture from 2 Timothy 3 is repeated through the Old Testament.

> "And now, O Israel, listen to the statutes and the rules that I am teaching you, and do them, that you may live, and go in and take possession of the land that the Lord, the God of your fathers, is giving you. You shall not add to the word that I command you, nor take away from it, that you may keep the commandments of the Lord your God that I command you." —Deuteronomy 4:1-2

> "Everything that I command you, you shall be careful to do. You shall not add to it or take from it." —Deuteronomy 12:32

> "Every word of God proves true; he is a shield to those who take refuge in him. Do not add to his words, lest he rebuke you and you be found a liar." —Proverbs 30:5-6

In these texts, God is proclaiming to us the doctrine of *sufficiency*. Not only is His Word true, it is enough. God gives us a strong warning not to take away from His words. We need all of them! Then on the other side, we have the divine warning not to add to His words. We don't need any more divine revelation than what we have. We must never be so arrogant as to mix our wisdom with God's. His Word is sufficient. He has declared it to be enough.[3]

Jesus Himself taught this doctrine. In the Sermon on the Mount, Jesus was speaking about the Scriptures God had given up to that point in history, the Old Testament.

> "Do not think that I have come to abolish the Law or the Prophets; I have not come to abolish them but to fulfill them. For truly, I say to you, until heaven and earth pass away, not an iota, not a dot, will pass away from the Law until all is accomplished." —Matthew 5:17-18

Jesus was preaching *sola Scriptura*! He wanted to make sure His hearers understood that to believe in Him meant believing all the Scriptures, and to believe in all the Scriptures, was to believe in Him.[4] There can be no separating believing in Jesus, and believing every word of His written revelation.

Some in the church today say we should focus our attention on the red letters. In many Bibles, the words of Jesus are written in red. Most of my life, I have used "red letter edition" Bibles. Despite the fact that this is a helpful way for us to find Jesus' teaching in the New Testament, we must remember this was not God's idea. When the Holy Spirit was inspiring John to write his Gospel, He did not say, "OK for this next paragraph, put down that black pen, and pick up the red one."

Jesus' words above stand diametrically opposed to a thought process that puts the red letters above all the others. If we really wanted to be consistent in writing all of Jesus' words in red, we would have to print the whole Bible in red. The Bible is the divine Word of our triune God. He is the Author of every word, and Jesus wanted to make it clear to us that we needed every one—no more, no less.

Death in the Ditches

Perhaps you have heard the phrase, "There are two ways we can fall off on this." The doctrine of the sufficiency of Scripture is a narrow path that leads to pleasing God in all things, but there are deep ditches on both sides. These ditches are the detours to sin and death. On one side is the ditch of rebellion, on the other side the ditch of legalism.

I believe the ditch of rebellion is easier to see. Do you remember the warnings from Deuteronomy and from Jesus not to "take away" any words of the Bible? This is a warning against rebellion. God has said do A, but I am going to do B. God has said not to do C, but I am going to do C. We can rebel in both our thoughts and our actions. When we deliberately think or act contrary to God's revealed will in the Bible, that is rebellion. When we disregard any portion of Scripture, we have begun sliding down the steep slopes of rebellion.

One of the most surprising things I have learned as I have explored the doctrine of the sufficiency of Scripture is that there are more warnings in the Bible against adding to what God has said compared to the warnings against taking away. For whatever reason, the ditch of rebellion seemed like the big, scary one, with the sharp rocks and wolves waiting at the bottom. The other side, the ditch of legalism, was bad, sure, but certainly not as bad as rebellion…Right? Not according to God.

In the Scriptures we looked at above, we saw the repeated warning from God not to add to the words He has revealed to us in the Bible. This dire warning is repeated in the last chapter of the Bible as well.

> "I warn everyone who hears the words of the prophecy of this book: if anyone adds to them, God will add to him the plagues described in this book." —Revelation 22:18

When we take away from God's Word that is rebellion. When we add to God's Word that is legalism. This is going to be a major theme in our journey ahead. I am convinced that many churches today are filled with legalism, and they don't even know it!

Simply defined, legalism is creating human rules for righteous living, which are not in the Bible, and judging yourself and others by those human rules.[5] One of Satan's greatest victories in the modern church is his success in causing us to believe a false definition of legalism. Satan's definition of legalism is, "Taking the Bible seriously on every subject and trying to obey the Bible in every area."

Imagine meeting a Christian who says, "I am trying to obey God's Word in every area of my life. I want to rightly apply every moral principle and command I find to my life at home, my life at church, and my life at work…I want the Bible to direct my every thought and every action!"

Many Christians today would say that sounds "legalistic." The reality is there is not a single shred of legalism in the paragraph above. Legalism is not seeking to follow the Bible in every area of thought and life. Legalism is adding human rules and regulations on top of the Bible.[6]

The other great "success" Satan has had in this battle is causing the word "legalist" to become one of the worst insults in the Christian church. To be called a "legalist" is to be dismissed, demeaned, and discarded. So look at how crafty the devil is! First, he redefines "legalist" to mean "anyone who takes the Bible really seriously," and then he causes the word to become a powerful insult.

Forgive me as I reiterate this point, because we can't move forward without reclaiming this word from the devil's deception. A legalist is not someone who seeks to rightly obey and apply every word of the Bible to his or her life. A legalist is someone who disobeys the Bible by adding to the Bible human rules and regulations for thought, life, and morality, and proceeds to judge themselves and others by these rules. A legalist is not someone who places divine law above all else. A legalist is someone who places human law above all else.[7]

The early church continually had to beat back the subtle deceptions of legalism. A spirit of legalism attacked the church in the area of doctrine, worship practices, church structure, and ministry methodology. When the early church did things *their* way, when they did what was right in their own eyes, churches were filled with conflict and ministry was hindered. However, when they did things God's way, by following the commands and patterns for ministry He had given to them in His Word, that ministry flourished and the Gospel message accelerated.

This was at the heart of Paul's warning to the church at Corinth.

> "I have applied all these things to myself and Apollos for your benefit, brothers, that you may learn by us not to go beyond what is written, that none of you may be puffed up in favor of one against another. For who sees anything different in you? What do you have that you did not receive? If then you received it, why do you boast as if you did not receive it?" —1 Corinthians 4:6-7

Paul is pleading with them to give their full and undivided attention to God's revelation[8], as a final and sufficient guide for every area of Christian life, at church, at home, and in the marketplace. When legalism infects a church, the results are predictable. Leaders become prideful and divisions grow. This is the inevitable result when church decisions are made based on human wisdom, human creativity, and human innovation rather than the revealed Word of God.

Falling Both Ways At Once

As we have seen, there are two terrible ways we can fall away from the truth and sufficiency of God's Word. We can arrogantly ignore His words through rebellion, or we can arrogantly add to His words through legalism. In Genesis 3, Eve fell both ways at the same time.

> "Now the serpent was more crafty than any other beast of the field that the LORD God had made. He said to the woman, "Did God actually say, 'You shall not eat of any tree in the garden'?" And the woman said to the serpent, "We may eat of the fruit of the trees in the garden, but God said, 'You shall not eat of the fruit of the tree that is in the midst of the garden, neither shall you touch it, lest you die.'" —Genesis 3:1-3

In verse 3, Eve says something that gives us a clue something terrible has happened. She adds words to the command of God. The Lord never said anything about not touching the fruit. She has already begun the slide into legalism.

Then in verse 4, Satan tries to push her off the other side at the same time.

> "But the serpent said to the woman, 'You will not surely die.'" —Genesis 3:4

In the end, God's command was neither binding, nor enough. Adam failed to obey God's Word as well and this same battle has been waging ever since. Our sinful nature loves rebellion. Our sinful nature loves legalism. Most of all, we love to mix them together into a wicked mess which leads to death.

Legalism and the Reformation

In the previous chapter, we identified the sufficiency of Scripture as the root issue of the Protestant Reformation during the 14th-16th centuries. Which way had the Roman Catholic Church fallen, into the ditch of rebellion or legalism? Had the church taken away from what God had said, or had they added human wisdom and human regulations on top of the Bible? The answer is the latter. The greater issue was that the church was teaching that there were additional requirements, beyond what was written in the Bible, which were needed for salvation and for pleasing God. These new humanistic regulations included attendance at certain masses, repeatedly praying specific prayers, and enduring purgatory. Indulgences could be purchased to shorten the length of your suffering there as well as speed your loved ones on to Heaven. Prayers were to be offered to and for the dead. Mary was elevated to sinless status, and was deserving of worship along with Christ. These things, which are not found anywhere in Scripture, were added by the church to what it meant to live a faithful Christian life.

Because of their love for God's church, men like Luther and Calvin risked their lives to call the church back to *sola Scriptura*. Their intent was not to break away but to reform the church using the Bible alone. The reformation and the reformers were far from perfect. As Francis Schaeffer puts it, "The reformation was no golden age; and our eyes should not turn back to it as if it were to be our perfect model."[9] They had sin in their personal lives just as we do. The churches they eventually established had problems, just like our churches do. Nevertheless, they were striving to return to the practices of the early church, as described by God in the Bible.

If God has given instruction or direction to us in Scripture, church leaders are morally bound to encourage and call the congregation to obedience. If God has not given an instruction to us in Scripture, it is therefore not *necessary* for faithful Christian living. If God has not commanded it, the church must not require it.

The Guard Rail

I am so thankful God has chosen to reveal Himself, His will, and the true history of our world through the written revelation of the Bible. We would literally be lost without it.

How do we stay on the narrow path of following God's will in every sphere of life? How do we maintain sure footing and not fall into the temptation of rebellion on one side, or the temptation of legalism on the other?

God has not sent us out across a tightrope! Yes, the path is narrow, but on both sides of the path is a solid handrail, driven down deep into the rock. What has God given to us that we might not rebel against Him? He has given us His sufficient Word. What has God given us that we might not become legalists and elevate our words above His? He has given us His sufficient Word.

The handrail is the sufficiency of Scripture. Walking the path of the Christian life, without holding on to this railing is the height of foolishness. I have a lot of personal experience with this foolishness, as I will share in the pages ahead, and I don't ever want to go back. The mission God has entrusted to us is too important!

Questions for Discussion:

1. Do you agree we have a new kind of Christian in the world today who says, "I love Jesus, but I don't completely believe the Bible."? Why or why not?

2. In your life, are you more frequently tempted by the sin of rebellion (ignoring what God has said) or legalism (adding your own rules on top of what God has said)?

3. Do you see more rebellion or legalism in your local church? In your family? Why do you think this is?

4. Can you see any invasions of legalism in your church? Are there human programs or practices so "strongly encouraged" that people might feel guilty if they don't do them?

ENDNOTES

[1] Deuteronomy 29:29

[2] This question is worded in such a way as to adhere to the doctrine of "intentional" inerrancy. Each text of Scripture means what God, through the human author, intended it to mean. For instance, in Psalm 91:4 we read, "He will cover you with his pinions, and under his wings you will find refuge." Based on our study of this passage, do we conclude that it is the intention of the author to declare that God has literal feathers and wings? No, we would make the interpretive choice that God, through the human author, is using a metaphor that describes God's caring protection of His children.

[3] God provided each era of the Church with all the revelation it needed at that time. The Torah was completely sufficient for the Israelites in the wilderness. God then added to His revelation through the prophets, forming the entire Old Testament, which was sufficient for God's people until the time of Christ. With the work of Christ, new Scripture was given, completing the New Testament. What a blessed age we live in to have so many words from God! We can eagerly look forward to the expansion of divine revelation when Christ returns!

[4] As we will discuss later, we must seek to rightly interpret and apply what God has said. For instance, in the Old Testament God commands that animals be sacrificed. We do not "obey" that commandment today because

God tells us in the New Testament that the sacrificial system has been superseded by Christ and is no longer necessary.

[5]The term legalism is also sometimes used to refer to the doctrine of "works righteousness" or the belief that we can earn or merit our salvation through good deeds.

[6]There are two fundamental definitions of the word legalism. The first has to do with "works righteousness" or seeking to merit salvation with our good deeds. The second the focus of our discussion, which is the adding of human rules and regulations to the Bible, and judging oneself and others by those additional human rules.

[7]Jesus did not confront the Pharisees for seeking to be obedient to the Bible, but rather for adding human rules and regulations (legalism) on top of what God had said in His Word.

[8]At this point the church in Corinth had the Old Testament, and most likely some of the early writings of the New Testament. Clearly, they had the apostolic instruction from Paul contained in his letter.

[9]Francis Schaeffer, *How Should We Then Live* (Crossway, Wheaton, IL: 1976), 105.

CHAPTER 3

Every Good Work

"Your word is a lamp to my feet, and a light to my path."

—Psalm 119:105

Now let's take the first of many treacherous steps toward bringing together the sufficiency of Scripture with the mission God has given us to reach the world with the Gospel.

Think about this question for a moment. What is an example of a good work? See if you can quickly come up with five "good works." Consider jotting them down on a piece of paper or in the margin.

Now think about putting those good works into action. How would you (or someone else) go about doing the good works you came up with? How could those things not just be done, but also be done in a way that honors God? Let's return to God's words from 2 Timothy 3.

> "All Scripture is breathed out by God and profitable for teaching, for reproof, for correction, and for training in righteousness, that the man of God may be complete, equipped for every good work." —2 Timothy 3:16-17

In verse 16, as we learned in the last chapter, God uses clear and comprehensive language so we would understand we need all the words of His written revelation, no more, and no less, and that these words speak to every essential sphere of thought and action.

In verse 17, God applies His doctrine of the sufficiency of His Word to our ministry and mission in the world. We are called to advance His Gospel, build His Kingdom, and bring Him glory. We have myriad opportunities every day to do these things in our roles as children, spouses, employees, neighbors, parents, volunteers, and church leaders.

God makes a dramatic claim about the Bible at the end of verse 17. God claims that His written Word is able to make you complete, and to equip you for every good work. Do you want to be a complete parent? God's Word can thoroughly equip you. Do you want to be complete servant in your church? God's Word can thoroughly equip you.

If something is true, right, noble, pure, lovely, excellent, admirable, or praiseworthy, God says that the Bible will equip us for success. In the Bible, the Lord not only tells us what His will is, but how He wants His will carried out. He gives us His ends, and His means.

The NIV translation emphasizes this point.

> "All Scripture is God-breathed and is useful for teaching, rebuking, correcting and training in righteousness, so that the servant of God may be thoroughly equipped for every good work." —2 Timothy 3:16-17 (NIV)

Look back at your list of "good works." Do you believe the Bible can thoroughly equip you for every one of them? This presses us on whether or not we really believe in the doctrine of the sufficiency of Scripture. Is the Bible enough for us when it comes to what it means to be a husband, a mother, a women's ministry leader, or a preacher? Do we believe that in the Bible we have all we need to please God and grow His Kingdom?

The four levels of Scripture

God has given us four levels of truth in His Word. For much of my Christian life, I only saw the first two!

Level 1 – God's truth (Doctrine)

God has given us all the truth we need about who He is, who we are, life, death, Heaven, hell, and salvation. The list of essential truth could go on. I don't need to belabor this point, because you already agree! The Bible is sufficient for all matters of doctrine.

Level 2 – God's will (Righteousness)

Not only has God given us His truth in the Bible, He has given us His will. Every thought and action He requires, and every thought and action He forbids, is given to us in His Word.

Level 3 – God's ways (Methodology)

In the Scriptures, God not only tells us *what* to do, but *how* to do it. As I hope to demonstrate in the pages ahead, the Lord not only gives us His ways, but His means as well.

Level 4 – God's call (Jurisdiction)

Particular aspects of God's will are assigned to specific jurisdictions. God gives particular instructions to pastors, government leaders, children, parents, etc. So God not only reveals what He wants done, how it is to be done, but also who should do it.

Proper devotion

Consider the following illustration. Imagine a new believer comes to you seeking spiritual advice. He says, "I know God is a personal God, and He wants me to draw near to Him in worship." Your friend has just demonstrated a correct understand of God's revelation in regards to level one and level two—doctrine and righteousness. "God is a personal God," is a statement of biblical doctrine. "God wants me to draw near to Him in worship," is a true statement that reflects God's righteous will. So far, so good.

Your friend continues, "So in order to draw near to God, I am going to go up to the top of the mountain each morning, scrape myself with sharp rocks and jump in the fire. These are things that help me to worship God and feel close to Him."

How would you counsel your friend? I expect that you would affirm him for his desire to worship God, but would lovingly confront him on his proposed plan for worship. His doctrine was right. His understanding of God's will was correct. But when it came to *how* to do God's will, in this case *how* to worship Him, he departed from Scripture and chose his own path.

If God is a personal God, and wants us to draw near to Him in worship, *how* should we do that? Scripture is sufficient to answer the question of *methodology*. God calls us to pray, meditate on His Word, fast, worship Him with our families, worship Him with our church, etc. The believer is not simply called to believe the truth and seek to do God's will, but to do God's will, God's way.

Limiting the Bible

A tragic shift took place in some parts of 20th century Christianity, and many believers I know, including myself, were taken in by it. This was explained to me in the extraordinary book by Francis Schaeffer, *How Should We Then Live?*.[1] If you have not read the book, or watched the DVD series, I encourage you to do so. It is one of the best resources for Christians who want to relate to and minister to our broken world with grace and truth. The book traces the history of religion, philosophy, art, and culture, from the Roman Empire to the present day.

The shift, as Schaeffer explains it, had to do with how Christians during the 20th century changed the way they related to, understood, and applied the Bible. Look at the pictures below. In the center of the Bible, we have "religion." Here we find issues such as the nature of God, the nature of man, original sin, the person and work of Christ, the afterlife, etc. Then on the outer edges, you find "real" stuff like money, work, science, education, and church. It is here where we find the issues, roles, disciplines, and institutions we interact with on a daily basis.

The cataclysmic shift in the 20th century in many of our churches, hearts, and homes was removing the authority and sufficiency of the Bible from the outer circle, and restricting the authority of God's Word only to matters of "religion." So if a group of Christians today are discussing the question, "Who was Jesus?" They will use the Bible and the Bible alone. "How can we be saved?" Let's open the Bible and find out. "What is the role of the Holy Spirit?" God has answered this question for us in many different places in the Bible. When it comes to these "religious" questions, most Christians rely on Scripture, and Scripture alone, in their search for answers. However, the issues we face in daily life are effectively pushed beyond the authority of the Bible. The result of this shift in our culture, churches, and families has been devastating.

The Bible is Sufficient for History

History is important to God. It has become a bit cliché but is still true: History = His-Story. Therefore, we can have confidence that everything we need to know about the history of the world is in the Bible.

The Bible is not a *comprehensive* book of history. Many real events have taken place that are not recorded in the Old and New Testaments. But God has given us the true historical events, which He wants us to know and understand. He wants us to know about the true history of how our first parents brought sin into the world. He wants us to know the true history of God's judgment against sin through a global flood. He wants us to know the true history of the fragmentation of language at the Tower of Babel. He wants us to know the true history of how He led His people out of Egypt. You get the point. God made the choice that certain events in the history of His universe needed to be revealed and preserved for all people. The Bible is a sufficient guide to human history in that it contains everything God says we need to know in order to know Him, love Him, and follow Him faithfully.

If we want to understand history rightly, we must first understand and believe the God of the Bible is sovereign over all things, and He is working all things together for His glory. We must also understand and believe that the pinnacle of history this side of eternity centers on Christ's death and resurrection from the dead. Apart from these truths, which are revealed to us by God in the Bible, we cannot rightly understand history.

This is the point where Christians start squirming. Perhaps you have been reading up to this point, thinking, "Yeah, yeah, yeah, the Bible is true, the Bible is sufficient." But now we are talking about the Bible as a true and sufficient book for history? Wait a minute! Is the Bible really meant to be used that way? This is the question we must answer.

The Bible is Sufficient for Science

God created and ordered the physical universe. He gave us rational and inquisitive minds, and He commanded us to take dominion over the earth.

He wants us to study it, figure it out, and be a good steward of it. Science was God's idea, and He tells us everything we need to know about it in the Bible.

OK, Rob. Now you have gone off the deep end. First, you tell me that the Bible contains everything we need to know about history. Now you think we should use it as a textbook in science class.

Stay with me! In the chapters ahead, we are going to apply this ministry-transforming, Gospel-accelerating doctrine to family life and church life, and I need to use as many examples as I can to lay a solid foundation.

Just as the Bible is not a comprehensive record of human history, the Bible is not exhaustive on matters of science. You won't find microbiology in the Bible. You won't find details about quantum physics. What you will find is everything God says we *need* to know about the world He created, and everything we need to know about how to study it.

For starters, if you want to explore God's created discipline of science properly, you need to know that He created the world. The universe is not here by chance. Life did not evolve from non-life. There was no accidental "big bang."

If you want to engage in true science, and come to true conclusions, you need to understand that people are not animals, but we are in a separate category of creation. It is true that humans have biological similarities to mammals, but we are not animals. We are special, unique, and set apart. Why can we say such a thing? We can say this because we believe God wrote down the true history of how He created the world.

God also went out of His way to inspire Moses to write down the scientific and historical fact that animals and plants do not change from one species to another. God tells us, no fewer than five times in the first chapter of Genesis, that His creatures reproduce "according to their kinds."[2] Christianity and Darwinian evolution are totally incompatible with one another.

Again, the Bible only contains a small fraction of all available scientific knowledge. However, God has given us true, authoritative, divinely-revealed facts about His creation. God has given us what we *need* to know about His universe. The question is whether or not we will believe what He has revealed. The temptation of rebellion is calling! Just cut out some of God's words about how He created the world. No problem. It's not a big deal. The temptation to replace God's truth with man's truth is calling! You can believe the Bible and mix in some atheistic Darwinian evolution. No problem.

Look how confused our thinking has become. Atheistic science declares the resurrection to be impossible. Christians completely reject "science" on this point and declare the resurrection a historical fact. Atheistic science declares the virgin birth to be impossible. Again, Christians completely reject "science" and stand firm on the historical reality that the Holy Spirit alone was responsible for the conception of Jesus in Mary's womb. Why are Christians so unbending on these points of history? Because the Bible declares these things to be true! So why is it when atheistic science declares the creation timeline in Genesis to be impossible, do we become confused and weak-kneed about standing with faith and reason upon what God has said?

It is uncomfortable for Christians today to talk like this. We have been brainwashed into thinking the Bible has nothing to do with the outer circle (from the previous diagram). This was not the case for the reformation Christians. In fact, modern science was born and developed out of a biblical and distinctively Christian worldview. Men like Newton believed first and foremost the God of the Bible had created the world, and because this God was a God of order, His creation could be studied. They believed that scientific inquiry would yield results simply because a perfect God had made the world.

Few Christians will say it, but many act and think as if God's Word has nothing to do with real life. Sure, the Bible is a great book for religious stuff, but it can't help us out there in the world in which we live.

At this point, many will disagree with me and say it is not right to use the Bible like this. Did God mean to give us historical facts in the Bible? Did He mean to give us scientific facts in the Bible? Those are the million-dollar questions. You know what I think. What do you think? Where do you stand?

The Bible is Sufficient for the Family

The family was the first Gospel-advancing, Kingdom-building institution God created. The family is the foundation for all of human life, in all places, and in all times. Every person comes into the world through a father and a mother. It might be a broken family, adopted family, foster family, Christian family, or atheist family, but it is a family never the less.

God has created many roles within the family, and each of these roles is important in the eyes of God. Being a son or daughter is a divine calling, and it is a "good work." Being a sibling is a divine calling, and it is a "good work." God calls many into the role of husband or wife. Ministering to and with one's spouse is a "good work." God has blessed many of us with sons and daughters of our own, and we have therefore become fathers and mothers. Parenting and grand parenting are Great Commission callings, and therefore are "good works" of Christian ministry.

If something is important, as we would all agree family is, then we can be sure God's Word can thoroughly equip us for success and faithfulness.

God gives clear roles and responsibilities to husbands and to wives. He gives a clear mission to parents. He gives clear commands to sons, daughters, and siblings. Is the Bible a comprehensive guide on family life? No. It would be nice if there was a chapter on how best to do laundry and meal preparation for eight people. You may never be on top of the laundry, and the meals may never be gourmet, but your family can still be used by God to make disciples and grow His Kingdom. God has promised us in 2 Timothy 3:17 that His Word will thoroughly equip us for every good work, and this promise applies to the ministry God has called us to within our families.

God didn't create marriage simply for pleasure and companionship. It brings comfort but it is ultimately about covenant. It brings happiness but it is ultimately about holiness. Marriage is a Great Commission institution. It is a powerful discipleship relationship for the husband and for the wife, and together they are given the mission of making disciples of the next generation.

The mission of parenting and grand parenting is not to raise healthy kids who make a positive contribution to society. Parenting is a divine mission for the Kingdom of God! Christian parenting is at the heart of the Great Commission, and yet I have heard month-long sermon series on the Great Commission without any mention of parents "making disciples" of their own children.

The purpose of family

Consider this question. What is the purpose of family? Write down your answer in the margin or on a note pad.

I have posed this question to many Christians and church leaders. More often than not, there is an awkward pause following the question as their minds scramble for a spiritual-sounding answer.

Few churches have a theology of family, and as a result, their evangelism and discipleship ministries are largely ineffective. God created two institutions to build His Kingdom and advance His Gospel, the local church and the family. In many communities, the Great Commission is going full-tilt in the church building, and is barely on the radar screen for individuals and families in their neighborhoods.

Trying to reach a community for Christ without embracing God's plan for the local church and the local family to both engage in the Great Commission is like pedaling a bike with only one pedal. It is awkward, tiring, and very slow.

Repentance

This part of the discussion is deeply personal for me. For many years, I did not follow the simple instructions God gives to fathers. There are many Scriptures that speak to dads, but perhaps the clearest is Ephesians 6:4.

> "Fathers, do not provoke your children to anger, but bring them up in the discipline and instruction of the Lord."

The summer of 2004 was a dark summer. My wife, Amy, and I had been blessed with four children at that time. (We now have six!) I had been serving as a youth minister for over a decade. If you had asked me at that time what my priorities in life were as a Christian man, I would have responded quickly and with conviction, "My first priority in life is my personal relationship with God, followed by my love relationship with my wife. My kids come next, and my fourth priority is my ministry in the church." God, spouse, kids, others.

Not only did I preach about this prioritized Christian life, I lived it. If the phone rang and my boss was on the other line with a crisis, and at the same time the other phone rang and Amy was on the line with a crisis, where would I go? How would I respond? I would go home. In a crisis, I would not put my work ahead of my wife.

Over the course of that summer, the Holy Spirit began to press me with a difficult question. "What are your priorities if there is no crisis?" During a normal week, where did I give the best of my heart, passion, energy, leadership, and vision? When I considered my life in light of that question, I did not like what I saw. I preached the Christian life priorities of God, spouse, kids, and others, but in my everyday life, the order was completely backwards: others, kids, Amy, God. It sounds horrible to say it this way, but my heart was at my job. When I was at work, I was thinking about work. When I was at home, I was thinking about work. This was followed by my relationship with my children. I was not an absent father, physically or emotionally. I tried to spend time with them and connect with them personally. But I had no plan, whatsoever, to pass my faith on to my children. As a youth pastor, I had tremendous strategic plans to pass my faith on to everyone else's children! But with the immortal souls that God had entrusted to my care . . . I was just showing up. I gave them my spiritual leftovers after I poured myself out at work.

My next priority was my marriage to Amy. After I gave my best at work and gave the leftovers to the kids, Amy got what few scraps were left. This is not to say that I did not try to spend time with her and do what I could to help around the house, but my heart was not with her first and foremost.

I was seen as a strong spiritual leader at my church, while I was providing virtually no spiritual encouragement for my wife.

Because my life was upside down and backwards, I was also far from God . . . and I did not even know it. It was a dark summer because I had to admit that the life I thought I was living was a mirage. I was not a man who put my ministry to my wife and children first. God brought me to a place of brokenness and repentance. I confessed and acknowledged the broken state of my life to God and repented to my wife and children. Then God began graciously to rebuild my family on the sufficiency of His Word and His grand purpose for our lives. Now, eight years after the rebuilding began, our family continues to learn, grow, repent, and seek God together.[3]

The Bible is sufficient for the local church

God created the local church.[4] The local church was not a human invention. The disciples did not sit around after Christ's ascension and brainstorm the local church into existence. God instituted the church, with Christ as its head. The Holy Spirit inspired the apostles and the writers of the New Testament to build His church on specific structures and practices. Leading and serving our local church is a "good work" and God promises the Bible can thoroughly equip us for success.

God cares deeply about your church. He has created the Church in general and your local church in particular to advance His Gospel to the ends of the earth. Thankfully, He has not asked us to build our church on human wisdom, creativity, and innovation. In the Bible, God has given us everything we need to know about how His church is to function. As we will discover, God has entrusted the institution of the local church with a *limited* set of responsibilities and purposes. The local church is most effective, and brings God the greatest glory, when it fulfills the specific purposes God has given to it in the Bible—no less, and no more.

Pastoral repentance

For the first decade of my pastoral life, I had little to no understanding about the sufficiency of Scripture as it related to my leadership in the church. During those years, I was a youth pastor, and one of my favorite principles was, "I have an unchanging message in a constantly changing package." In other words, the message of the Gospel is unchanging, but my ministry methods will be constantly changing to meet the changing needs of youth culture. I was quite proud of how missiological this sounded! I felt I could and should do anything to evangelize and disciple the teens in my community.

But there was a terrible problem with this philosophy. When it comes to ministry in the local church, God is not silent on the method. The Bible doesn't say, "Here is the Gospel, get it to children however you want to." Instead, God's Word is filled with His ends *and* His means. He tells us what He wants and how He wants it done.

Remember that God has spoken to us on four levels in the Bible. I only saw the first two levels of "God's truth" and "God's will." I believed and embraced that the Bible taught God's love and heart for children (God's truth). I believed and embraced that in the Bible God expresses His will that children are to be evangelized and discipled (God's will). But, that was as far as I went. I completely missed His methods and His jurisdictions. I embraced God's ends, but not God's means.

In the Bible God not only tells us His heart to reach children for Christ, but He tells us how He wants it done. If you locked yourself in a room with the Bible and you asked the question, "God, how do you want young people to be evangelized and discipled?" what do you think the answer would be? What method has God given us to raise the next generation for the glory of God?

If you used the Bible and the Bible alone, the answer would be overwhelmingly clear. God created parents and grandparents to be the primary spiritual trainers of their children at home. God created parents and grandparents to shepherd and disciple their children. This is the divine strategy for next generation ministry.

Despite the fact God has spoken so clearly about this in the Bible, I created a youth ministry where parents could drop their kids off with me and the other "professionals" so we could teach them the Bible, equip them for ministry, pray with them, and keep them accountable.

In the same way I had to repent of my lack of following the Bible in my life at home, I had to repent in my professional life at church. When it came to ministry decisions, I was doing things my way, in my wisdom, with my innovations, and through my creativity. I had to repent of the fact I was leading an unbiblical ministry. This is not to say everything I was doing was sinful, but when it came to my youth ministry, I was not allowing the Bible to determine my methods.

I believe that ministering to children and youth is a "good work!" Therefore, I believe in the Bible God has given us everything we need to be successful. For a more detailed discussion of the sufficiency of Scripture and youth ministry visit the church leadership page at www.visionaryfam. com.

Not only is the Bible sufficient for youth ministry, but for every "good work of the church." When we believe this—it changes everything.

- Do you believe the Bible is sufficient for women's ministry in your church?
- Do you believe the Bible is sufficient to direct your church in how you care for the poor?
- Do you believe the Bible is all you need to develop a strategy to minister to singles?
- Do you believe the Bible is sufficient to teach us how we are to worship God?

The easy answer is, "yes!" But how often is the Bible open in your ministry planning sessions? Are your leadership decisions based on what you think will work best, what seems most creative, or what God has specifically said in His Word? Do you seek to make every ministry decision in light of the commands and patterns for the New Testament church? God has spoken clearly and directly about every necessary ministry in His church, but are we listening? More importantly, are we seeking to be obedient to what He has said?

Right in our Own Eyes

The book of Judges is one of the saddest books in the Bible. There is a refrain that runs through the chapters, "Everyone did what was right in his own eyes."[5] For many of my years as a pastor, this phrase described how I made ministry decisions. I did what I thought was best. My team and I made decisions about what we thought would be most effective. Pragmatism, not God's Word, far too often was the driving principle.

A few years ago I spoke at a Christian high school weekend retreat. They asked me to preach on John 15, the passage where Jesus teaches about the vine and the branches. Jesus' primary call to His disciples in that passage is that they "abide in me." Jesus begins to explain what this means in verse 7 when He says, "If you abide in me and my words abide in you . . ." Then in verse 10 He makes it plain, "If you obey my commands, you will abide in my love." We spent the weekend talking about the importance of giving our best to obeying God's Word—the Bible.

At the end of the retreat, we had a question-and-answer session. A young man asked me a great question: "Can you be a Christian and not go to church? I don't like going to church." A group of students around this young man seemed to share his sentiments. I began my answer this way: "I appreciate your honesty, and I can understand your feeling disconnected in your church. I don't want to be offensive, but I do want to answer your question in a straight-forward way. If a person claims to be a follower of Jesus, and is not faithfully involved in the local church, then he or she is a disobedient Christian. I can't comment on anyone's salvation, but in Hebrews 10:25 God says that we should 'not give up meeting together, as some are in the habit of doing.'"

The young man responded, "I get that, but we don't like our church. Here's what we want to do. We're going to meet at our friend's house every Friday night, sing some songs, pray, and talk about Jesus. Our youth pastor told us that church was all about encouraging each other spiritually, so that's what we want to do. What do you think about that?"

I replied, "Wow! I love what you're talking about. You're committing to meet every Friday night with your friends to focus on spiritual growth together? That's terrific and I admire that. I do have a couple questions for you. First, will there be preaching of the Bible when you meet?"

"No."

"Will you have baptisms?"

"No."

"Will you have communion?"

"No."

"Will you have multiple, biblically-qualified elders there?"

"No."

"Again, I don't have anything negative to say about your meeting every week like you described. It sounds wonderful. But . . . it's not a church. Church is not man's idea. We didn't think it up. Church is God's idea. He's the one who instituted it, and He is the one who gave us, in the Scriptures, the specific patterns and practices that He wants for it."

"Well, Pastor Rob, where does it say in the Bible that you have to have elders?"

At this point, I confess . . . I got lucky. I likely wouldn't have known the answer to that question off the top of my head. But God knew that this question would come my way this weekend, and so a few days earlier I "just happened" to be reading in the book of Titus. So I replied, "In Titus 1:5, Paul instructs the church that the first thing they were to do is appoint elders in every town."

At that moment, the young man responded with a question I'll never forget. He said, "How about another one?" In other words, do you have *another* Bible passage that supports what you're saying? My heart fell inside of me, and I quietly said, "I didn't know I needed more than one."[6]

This was a retreat with students who professed faith in Christ. I realized in that moment this young man and I were not having a disagreement about the nature of church—but rather a disagreement about the nature of the

Bible. This young man, like many of his Christian peers, did not view the Bible as a sufficient guide for every matter of faith and life—in this case, the particular nature and function of the church.

He'd asked me a question. I answered his question with a plain Scripture. To my dismay, it wasn't enough to change his mind, nor the minds of many around him. The Bible alone was not enough for him in regards to how the local church should function.

This is one of the great crises facing the church today. We have a generation of young people who, while they may have been taught the doctrine of inerrancy, and would say they believe "the Bible is true," have never been taught the doctrine of sufficiency. It is one of the key reasons why we are losing the majority of our children to the world.

Now is the time to return to the Bible alone for every matter of faith and practice!

Questions for Discussion:

1. Why do you think there is often tension and conflict when someone brings the Bible into "the outer circle," i.e. into conversations about history, government, marriage, etc?

2. Can you think of examples in the Bible where God tells us both what He wants and how He wants it done?

3. In your experience in the local church, is there a greater emphasis on pragmatism (what will be most effective?) or God's Word (what has God said about this particular ministry in His Word?)

4. What part of this chapter did you most agree with? What part did you most struggle with?

ENDNOTES

[1]Francis Schaeffer, *How Should We Then Live* (Wheaton, IL: Crossway, 1983).

[2]Genesis 1:11, 12, 21, 24, and 25

[3]Rob Rienow, *Visionary Parenting* (Nashville, TN: Randall House, 2009).

[4]When I speak of "the church" in this book, I am referring specifically to "the local church." There is, of course, the "church universal" which includes all believers on earth at a given period of time, as well as those believers who are already home with the Lord. When I talk about "the mission of the church" and "God's will for His church" I am focusing on God's specific will for His institution of the local church.

[5]Judges 17:6

[6]Rob Rienow, When They Turn Away (Grand Rapids, MI: Kregel, 2010).

CHAPTER 4

A Dangerous Doctrine

"So the word of the Lord continued to increase and prevail mightily."

—Acts 19:20

Make no mistake! The doctrine of the sufficiency of Scripture is a dangerous doctrine. While God's Word will perfectly guide you toward pleasing Him and living out the Great Commission, it will also lead you into great difficulty, challenge…even suffering and persecution.

Danger to our pride

In chapter 1, we briefly looked at the five "*solas*" of the Protestant Reformation:

- Only Scripture
- Only grace
- Only faith
- Only Christ
- Only for the glory of God

On the surface, these five words seem harmless enough. In fact, within the church, they might even feel a little dull. The Bible, grace, faith, Jesus, God…I've heard all that before.

The reality is these five "onlys" are the reason why biblical Christianity is so offensive to our pride, and to the world apart from Christ.

Let's think about "only grace." According to Ephesians 2:1, we enter the world dead in our trespasses and sins. We have no hope of approaching God, or reconciling ourselves to Him. Dead people are just that, dead. How incredibly offensive! Our sinful nature cries out, "Don't tell me I'm dead. Don't tell me I can't approach God."

What about "only faith?" In Ephesians 2, God goes on to say we cannot do enough good things to earn God's favor and earn His forgiveness. We can't pull ourselves up to Heaven by our bootstraps. Instead, the only path to salvation is to admit we can't save ourselves. All we can do is believe in what Christ accomplished through His death and resurrection. We are saved by grace alone, through faith alone…so that no one can boast. Human pride is completely confronted and utterly destroyed.

The nuclear attack on our pride continues with "only Christ." I don't know about you, but I like to do things my way. I am happy to do something for you, just let me do it the way I want to do it. God comes to man and says I have made one and only one way for you to be saved from hell, and that is through my Son, Jesus Christ. He has the supremacy in all things, and He is the only way. Take it or leave it.

To make matters worse, we come to "only for the glory of God." The end of all things is not fame for me, but fame for God. It is not about me, it's about Him.

Lastly, we have the foundation upon which all the other doctrines rest, "only Scripture." It is here God seeks to deal the deathblow to pride. The doctrine of the sufficiency of Scripture requires me to say, "I am not smart enough to know the difference between right and wrong. I am not wise enough to figure out how to please God. My reason is fallen and inadequate. The only chance I have of thinking rightly and understanding truth is through God's revelation to me in His written Word."

If we chose to believe in the truth and sufficiency of the Bible, God will lovingly and ruthlessly deal with the pride in our hearts. This is part of His perfect plan to mold us into the image of His Son.

Danger to our standing in the world

Choosing to believe in the truth and sufficiency of the Bible is not the path to popularity. It is quite the opposite.

> "For the word of the cross is folly to those who are perishing, but to us who are being saved it is the power of God." —1 Corinthians 1:18

Christianity is built on a pre-modern worldview. Even writing that feels embarrassing. Much has been said about our current age of post-modernism. In a post-modern worldview, the ultimate authority for what is true, right, noble, and good is me, my feelings, and my experience. I am the ultimate arbiter of truth. Therefore, I can have my truth; you can have yours, etc. If it feels good to me, then it is good for me.

You don't have to look far to find Christians decrying the evils of post-modernism and its destructive effects on the souls of this generation. However, some of these critiques seem to imply, "If only we could return to the modern view of the world, which was supportive and compatible with biblical Christianity."

But what is the ultimate authority for what is true, right, noble and good in the modern worldview? *Human reason* is the arbiter of truth for the modern mind. If it can be studied, examined, repeated, and made to submit to logic, then we can believe it.

The Christian rejects the worldview of this age (post-modernism) and the worldview of the previous age (modernism). We do not believe our feelings and personal experience determine truth for ourselves or for anyone else. We also don't believe our human reason is the ultimate measure of all things.[1] Instead, we believe our experience, feelings, reason, and logic are all fallen and thus potentially dangerous.

So where does that leave us? As followers of Christ, we embrace a pre-modern path to ultimate truth. My feelings will not lead me to the truth. My experience will not lead me to the truth. My reason will not lead me to the truth. I need supernatural revelation from God. God has graciously revealed His truth, for all people, in all places, and in all times, in the Bible.

God calls His children to stand up and declare, "Our experiences, feelings, and reason are unreliable. We must rely on the Word of God alone." To utter such things is a sure path to ridicule and rejection from the world.

Play it safe?

There are two ways to avoid this criticism and rejection. Not only will these two action steps help you to avoid ridicule, you may actually earn the world's praise.

1. Always speak of the Bible as being on the same level with other religious books.

You might say something like, "There are many valuable religious books in the world, but for me, I have found that the Bible is the one which has helped me the most."

This enables you to have a religious conversation with little or no offense to anyone else. The problem with this, of course, is that to take this position is to fully embrace the post-modern worldview along with its rejection of absolute truth. "I choose to believe the Bible because it connects the best with my experience."

2. Never bring the Bible into any conversation about real life.

The other way for a Christian to minimize the world's ridicule is to avoid bringing the Bible into any practical conversation. If you are talking with friends about a political issue, don't bring up any of the things God says about government in the Bible. If you are wrestling with a business decision, keep clear of the Scriptures that speak to economics. Be absolutely sure never to bring up the Bible in the context of any discussion of sexuality!

As long as your "Bible talk" stays in the church, and is restricted to religious stuff like Jesus, heaven, and trying to be a good person, you should be safe.

There is a path of safety, and many church attendees are on it. You won't face spiritual battles if you say, "I believe the Bible." But if you say, "I believe the Bible alone, as the final authority in all matters of faith and life," you will immediately be in enemy territory. This is our calling! It is in enemy territory where the great battles are won or lost.

Many men and women have died for their unwavering belief in the sufficiency of the Bible.[2] And we are not just talking about ancient history here. Martyrs are falling today because they will not give up their trust in the Word of God.

Consider God's words as given through the Apostle Paul:

> "Therefore, having this ministry by the mercy of God, we do not lose heart. But we have renounced disgraceful, underhanded ways. *We refuse to practice cunning or to tamper with God's word,* but by the open statement of the truth we would commend ourselves to everyone's conscience in the sight of God.[3] And even if our Gospel is veiled, it is veiled to those who are perishing. In their case the god of this world has blinded the minds of the unbelievers, to keep them from seeing the light of the gospel of the glory of Christ, who is the image of God. For what we proclaim is not ourselves, but Jesus Christ as Lord, with ourselves as your servants for Jesus' sake. For God, who said, "Let light shine out of darkness," has shone in our hearts to give the light of the knowledge of the glory of God in the face of Jesus Christ.
>
> But we have this treasure in jars of clay, to show that the surpassing power belongs to God and not to us. We are afflicted in every way, but not crushed; perplexed, but not driven to despair; persecuted, but not forsaken; struck down, but not

destroyed; always carrying in the body the death of Jesus, so that the life of Jesus may also be manifested in our bodies. For we who live are always being given over to death for Jesus' sake, so that the life of Jesus also may be manifested in our mortal flesh. So death is at work in us, but life in you." —2 Corinthians 4:1-12

The early Christians faced persecution because they *refused to tamper* with God's Word!

Danger to our standing in the church

Most Christians understand that following Christ means swimming upstream, against the flow of the godless culture around us. The early Christians were encouraged to take joy in their rejection, because it was a validation and confirmation of their obedience to Christ.[4]

While God calls us to take encouragement from persecution, it can be deeply hurtful, especially when we experience rejection and ridicule from members of our own family who are not believers.

It is one thing to experience rejection from the world because of our commitment to the Bible, but as awful as it sounds, we may experience rejection in our churches as well.

How can this be? Our local church is supposed to be a gathering of people who share our faith, beliefs, convictions, and worldview. This was Paul's prayer and encouragement for the church in Rome.

"For whatever was written in the former days was written for our instruction, that through endurance and through the encouragement of the Scriptures we might have hope. May the God of endurance and encouragement grant you to live in such harmony with one another, in accord with Christ Jesus, that together you may with one voice glorify the God and Father of our Lord Jesus Christ." —Romans 15:4-6

How could these believers be unified in spirit and mission? They could be unified because they had the Bible. They had the instruction and encouragement of the Scriptures to ground them in God's truth and direct them to God's will in all things.

It was this same unity the leaders of the Reformation wanted to see in the churches of their day. Here is how Francis Schaeffer described them:

> The Reformers turned not to man as beginning only from himself, but to the original Christianity of the Bible and the early church. Gradually they came to see that the church founded by Christ had since been marred with distortions. However, in contrast to the Renaissance humanists, they refused to accept the autonomy of human reason, which acts as though the human mind is infinite, with all knowledge within its realm. Rather, they took seriously the Bible's own claim for itself—that it is the only final authority.[5]

Post-modernism in the Church

So how is it possible for a Christian to face resistance and even ridicule in his or her own church for holding to the doctrine of the sufficiency of Scripture? The reason is because the humanist philosophies of post-modernism and modernism have subtly and successfully infiltrated many of our churches.

What are the signs of this infiltration? If post-modernist philosophy has crept into a church, there will be increasing elevation of personal experience as the benchmark of spiritual life. It is the Christian version of, "if it feels good, it is good." This manifests itself in many different ways.

Church members begin to measure their walk with God based on how close they feel to Him, rather than on their trust in Christ and obedience to the Bible. People then begin to question the assurance of their salvation because of their on-again off-again *feeling* of closeness to God. When this takes root in a church, there is a constant search and emphasis on creating programs, events, and environments designed to elicit this emotional response. Emotional responses to programs become the benchmark by which ministry is judged.

There is an increasing divide between a person's church life and "real life." I have vivid memories of youth group worship events with the room packed with hundreds of students, hands raised, passionately singing praise to God. Then ten minutes after the event was over, these same students would jump in their cars, spin their tires in the parking lot, and recklessly speed away down the street. Students would later say that the worship event was "awesome" and "I felt so close to God." Was God at work in the hearts and minds of the students at these events? I believe He was, but the disconnect between our worship gatherings and "real life" was obvious and discouraging.

To the degree post-modernism infects a church, moral decisions are increasingly made on personal feeling rather than the Bible alone. I have lost track of the number of times I have heard a man or woman tell me they had decided to divorce their spouse. As a pastor, I would share my deep sorrow for their pain, try to understand how they reached that decision, and see if there was a path to reconciliation. In many of these sad conversations, I discovered there was no abandonment, physical abuse, or adultery. So how could this faithful, long-time member of the church be choosing divorce? This is what I heard, time and time again, "Pastor Rob, I have prayed long and hard about this. I know God wants me to be happy. I have felt a sense of release from the Holy Spirit that this is the right thing for me to do. I can't really explain it, other than to say that I know God is OK with this." I don't want in any way to minimize the pain and suffering my friend was going through. My father was divorced four times, and my mother twice. My concern is that replacing our feelings with Scripture is an even greater crisis than the rising divorce rate!

Children in church?

Not only do feelings and personal experience increasingly drive moral decisions, but church decisions as well. In the book series ahead, we will seek to apply the doctrine of the sufficiency of Scripture to the practical life of the local church. One of the many questions we will tackle is "Do children belong in the corporate worship service?" It is an important question and there are strong opinions on all sides.

In 2005, Children's Ministry Magazine did a major article entitled "Where Should Children Worship?"[6] It was a "two perspectives" article in which a pair authors offered their convictions on the question. One argued for children being included in the corporate worship service, the other that children would worship best in a worship service designed just for them. It was a well-written and interesting article, and I don't mean to be personally critical of the authors. But what leaped off the pages to me was that there was no reference to the Bible's teaching on the subject![7] Each position was argued from the writer's personal and professional experience.[8]

Here was a major issue of discipleship on the table, and what were we counting on to guide us toward the will of God? Feelings, convictions, intuition, and personal experiences.

Will you face persecution in your church if you hold to the doctrine of the sufficiency of Scripture? To the degree your church has been infected with post-modern philosophy, absolutely. But if we are serious about living missional, externally-focused, Great Commission lives we must hold firmly to everything God has said about sanctification, morality, and the function of the local church.

Modernism in the Church

Just as post-modern philosophy can corrupt a local church, so can the worldview and values of modernism. As noted above, the final arbiter and guide for truth in the modern worldview is human reason. The action principle that emerges from this foundation is pragmatism.

On a personal level, when modernism rules a believer's life a spirit of Pharisaism is usually not far behind. It is possible for a person's head to be filled with knowledge of the Bible, but they do not believe it or act upon it.

> "Woe to you, scribes and Pharisees, hypocrites! For you are like whitewashed tombs, which outwardly appear beautiful, but within are full of dead people's bones and all uncleanness. So you also outwardly appear righteous to others, but within you are full of hypocrisy and lawlessness." —Matthew 23:27-28

So a man in the church can ace a "doctrine test," but he is not reading the Bible with his children at home. A teenager has all the answers in her small group Bible study, but she is sexually promiscuous. A woman can explain the four spiritual laws, but she is neglecting her aging parents.

Jesus told a parable of four soils, four different kinds of people responding to the Word of God. What made the good soil good? Why did the good soil produce a crop?

> "But those that were sown on the good soil are the ones who hear the word and accept it and bear fruit, thirtyfold and sixtyfold and a hundredfold." —Mark 4:20

According to Jesus, two fundamental things are required for us to bear fruit for Him. First, we must hear the Word. Second, we must accept the Word. Hearing the Bible in church each week and reading it at home during personal devotions and family worship is not enough. We must believe the words we are hearing and reading are the very words of God, and therefore seek to apply them to every area of our lives.

"But be doers of the word, and not hearers only, deceiving yourselves. For if anyone is a hearer of the word and not a doer, he is like a man who looks intently at his natural face in a mirror. For he looks at himself and goes away and at once forgets what he was like. But the one who looks into the perfect law, the law of liberty, and perseveres, being no hearer who forgets but a doer who acts, he will be blessed in his doing." —James 1:22-25

The spirit of pragmatism

On a church level, when the spirit of modernism is allowed access, staff meetings are increasingly filled with the question, "What will work best?" The base principles sound like, "We can and should do anything we possibly can to reach people for Christ. We need to be more creative. We need to be more innovative."

Imagine your pastoral team is discussing the previously mentioned question, "What should we do with children in regards to the weekly worship service?" Where would that conversation lead?

With post-modern values many of the comments will begin with, "In my experience," or "When I was growing up," and "For my family we have found..." When modernism drives the conversation sentences begin with, "I think it will be most effective if," or "It works better when," and "It makes the most sense to..."

My purpose here is not to bash experience or reason. God gives us both, and there is a proper use for them. But if we believe in the truth and sufficiency of the Bible, we do not base our personal, family, or church decisions on our experience or pragmatism. Instead, we diligently search the Bible, to discover what God has already said about the issues at hand.

So the question is on the table, "Do kids belong in church?" God would have our response begin with, "Let's open our Bibles and see what God has said about this in His Word. What pattern and commands do we find on this particular issue in the Scriptures and in the early church?"

Double Trouble

For most of us as individual Christians, and in our local churches, we are far more infected by post-modernism and modernism than we realize. We become twisted and governed by a bizarre mix of feelings, personal experience, human wisdom, and pragmatism, rather than the Scriptures.

There is a great risk for a church leader in standing on Scripture alone. It is one thing for the world to call us "Bible-bangers" and an entirely other thing for that accusation to come from our brothers and sisters in Christ.

If you seek to embrace and apply the sufficiency of Scripture in the life of your church, one response you can count on is being called a legalist. But as we explored earlier, this is a warped application of the word. A legalist is someone who does not believe the Bible is sufficient, and so they add additional human rules and regulations for morality and church life on top of what God has said. Legalism is an archenemy of the doctrine of the sufficiency of Scripture! Sadly, this is the word often used to dismiss and minimize those who want to try and humbly apply God's revelation to every area of life.

The path ahead

We must do three things if we want to have the Word of God be a lamp to our feet and a light to our path.[9]

1. We commit to using the Bible rightly.

Seeking to apply the doctrine of the sufficiency of Scripture requires we do all we can to properly interpret the Bible. This is not a comprehensive book on principles of Bible interpretation, but I hope they come through on every page.

I believe the Bible is its own interpreter. When we find a difficult passage on a particular subject, the first thing to do is to look for other passages on the same subject, which can bring clarity.

Great abuse takes place in the church when we use secondary texts, at the expense of primary texts, in determining doctrine and making practical decisions. This kind of misuse of God's Word is rampant.

Here are some examples, which I hope will clarify this point. Let's consider the question, "Is homosexual behavior right or wrong?"[10] There are many primary texts in the Bible that directly answer this question. One would be:

> "For this reason God gave them up to dishonorable passions.
> For their women exchanged natural relations for those that

are contrary to nature; and the men likewise gave up natural relations with women and were consumed with passion for one another, men committing shameless acts with men and receiving in themselves the due penalty for their error." —Romans 1:26-27

However, during the past 20 years in particular, another Scripture has been suggested as a more helpful response to this question:

"There is neither Jew nor Greek, there is neither slave nor free, there is no male and female, for you are all one in Christ Jesus." —Galatians 3:28

This verse has been used to declare that God sanctions and approves of homosexual behavior. This is a gross violation of the primary text/secondary text principle. The many primary texts, the ones that speak directly and clearly to the issue of homosexual behavior, are ignored, while a secondary text, which in this case has nothing to do with sexual behavior at all, is used to validate and support the person's opinion. With this principle in mind:

- When we are talking about youth ministry, we need to look at the specific Scriptures in which God speaks to the evangelism and discipleship of children and youth.
- When we are discussing the ministry of marriage, we turn to the specific instructions God has given to husbands and wives.
- When we are discussing our worship services, we need to look at the specific Scriptures where God instructs us how He wants us to worship Him.
- When we are wrestling with our strategy for women's ministry, we need to look at the specific Scriptures where God gives us His direction for how women are to minister to one another.

2. We commit to following the example of the Bereans.

In the book of Acts, the Gospel first spread among the Jews. In Acts 17, Paul and Silas travel to the town of Berea. Shortly after they arrived, they went to the synagogue and began to preach from the Old Testament that Jesus was the promised Messiah. How did the Bereans respond?

> "Now these Jews were more noble than those in Thessalonica; they received the word with all eagerness, examining the Scriptures daily to see if these things were so. Many of them therefore believed, with not a few Greek women of high standing as well as men."—Acts 17:11-12

Paul was speaking radical words to the Bereans. He was making outrageous claims. How could the Bereans test Paul's words? How could they discern if Paul was speaking from his own human wisdom or speaking the truth of God? Simple, they examined the Scriptures[11] to see if Paul's claims were indeed true. They knew they could completely trust God's written revelation in the Bible. If Paul's words matched up with God's then they would accept Paul's words. If not, they would reject them.

We should follow the example of the Bereans. How can you determine if what an author, a preacher on TV, or your pastor says is really true? Simple, examine the Scriptures to see if their words match up with God's. What measure can you use to judge and evaluate the words I have written in this book? Evaluate them against the Bible, and the Bible alone. One of my prayers is that this book series will cause God's book to be opened more than ever before!

Where will we find wisdom and guidance for the practical decisions that must be made in our homes and churches? Let us stand with the prophet Isaiah and answer, "To the teaching and to the testimony!"[12]

Perhaps you have heard that it is rude to answer a question with a question. But this is exactly what followers of Jesus Christ must do each and every day. When we face difficult questions, we must quickly ask, "What has God said about this in His Word?"

It is possible for two whole-hearted followers of Jesus Christ to seek direction from the Bible and arrive at two different interpretations. God will most certainly straighten out all of my wrong beliefs, interpretations, and doctrines when I enter eternity. While I have deep convictions about what the Bible teaches, I don't claim that my interpretation or my conclusions are inspired. Brothers and sisters in Christ will have honest disagreements about God's intended meaning in particular passages of Scripture. But let these disagreements never arise from a lack of humble and diligent study.

We need to be prepared and accept the reality that one believer may say, "I have become convinced these particular passages of Scripture instruct us to organize the church this way," and another says, "I have become convinced these particular passages of Scripture instruct us to organize the church that way." The beauty here is that both are seeking to humbly and honestly apply God's Word to the situation at hand. We may not always have unity on our conclusions, but let us always have unity on our commitment to the sufficiency of God's Word for every matter of faith and life!

3. We prepare to stand alone.

If you choose to follow the path of the sufficiency of Scripture for every matter of faith and practice, it may become a lonely journey. You will be choosing a path that is in radical opposition to the secular culture around you, as well as in opposition to any post-modern or modern philosophies in your church. You will be following the path of the Apostle Paul, who said,

> "For am I now seeking the approval of man, or of God? Or am I trying to please man? If I were still trying to please man, I would not be a servant of God." —Galatians 1:10

Faithfulness is worth it. Obedience is worth it. Doing what God wants, and doing it His way is worth it. God has spoken in His Word to every important matter of faith and life. He has given us in the pages of Scripture everything we need to worship Him rightly, please Him fully, and fulfill the Great Commission He has entrusted to us.

> If I profess with the loudest voice and clearest exposition every portion of the truth of God except precisely that point which

the world and the devil are at that moment attacking, I am not confessing Christ, however boldly I may be professing him. Where the battle rages, there the loyalty of the soldier is proved, and to be steady on all the battlefield besides is mere flight and disgrace if he flinches at that point.[13]

—Martin Luther

Questions for Discussion:

1. Which of the "sola" doctrines has God recently used in your life to deal with your pride?

2. Have you ever experienced rejection or ridicule from non-believers because of your belief in the Bible?

3. Have you ever experienced rejection or ridicule from believers because of your belief in the Bible?

4. Do you see any signs of post-modern or modern philosophies infecting your church?

5. What examples have you experienced of Christians misusing the Bible, and as a result, abusing people?

6. How would your local church change if it more closely followed the model of the New Testament church? What practical steps could you take to move your church in that direction?

ENDNOTES

[1]Thomas Aquinas (1225-1274) contributed to a tragic shift in the church during the late middle-ages. Aquinas, borrowing heavily from Aristotelian philosophy, redefined the biblical doctrine of original sin by suggesting that mankind fell morally, but not intellectually. He believed human reason had not been damaged by sin. This accelerated the influence of humanism in the church. This increasing humanism in the church was the primary driving force behind the reformers and their quest to see the church return to the doctrine of "Scripture alone." Francis Schaeffer's *How Should We Then Live*, as noted below, provides a solid historical overview for this critical period in world history.

[2]William Byron Forbush, Ed., Fox's Book of Martyrs: A History of the Lives, Sufferings, and Deaths of the Early Christians and Protestant Martyrs (Grand Rapids, MI: Zondervan, 1978).

3Italics mine

[4]1 Peter 1:6-7, James 1:2-4

[5]Francis Schaeffer, *How Should We Then Live* (Wheaton, IL: Crossway, 1983), 81.

[6]http://www.childrensministry.com/articles/where-should-children-worship

[7]Debbie Rowley made reference to Psalm 46:10 and Matthew 21, but neither of these passages are in any way related to the issue of children being a part of the corporate worship service of the church.

[8]For a Scriptural survey on the question of children and worship, consider the article *Do Children Belong in Church? http://visionaryfam.com/church-leaders/*

[9]Psalm 119:105

[10]This is not the same question as, "How should Christians respond to friends and family struggling with homosexuality?" but rather a straightforward question regarding the morality of the behavior in the eyes of God.

[11]The Bereans would have only had the Old Testament at this point.

[12]Isaiah 8:20a

[13]Luther's Works. Weimar Edition. Briefwechsel [Correspondence], vol. 3, pp. 8

THE JOURNEY AHEAD

My prayer is that you have been challenged and encouraged to deepen your study and commitment to the Bible as fully sufficient for every matter of faith and practice. I also pray your mind is filled with eager questions of application! If Scripture is sufficient for our ministry methods, what will that look like in our families and churches today?

I invite you to visit me online at www.visionaryfam.com to keep the conversation going. Through a series of books and articles we will explore:

- The sufficiency of Scripture
- The lost doctrine of jurisdiction
- God's mission for the family
- God's mission for the local church
- Uniting church and family in the Great Commission

Again, thanks for beginning this journey with me. My prayers are with you, with your family, and with your church, as you seek to love the Lord your God with all your heart, with all your soul, and with all your strength.

God's Love,

Rob Rienow

EVERY MARRIAGE
MATTERS TO GOD.

After years of counseling engaged and married couples, the Rienows realized that most Christian couples didn't know WHY God had brought them together! *Visionary Marriage* will reveal that God does have a plan and a purpose for marriage and family in the Bible. The focus is on the big-picture purpose for marriage, and the goal of being successful once understanding the purpose.

Ideal for small group study with discussion questions at the end of each chapter.

Visionary Marriage by Rob and Amy Rienow $12.99
Group discounts available

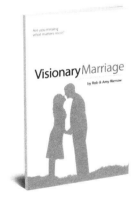

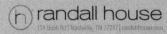

D6 Devotional Magazines
for the entire family!

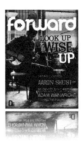

D6 Devotional Magazines are unique because they are the only brand of devotional magazines where the entire family studies the same Bible theme at the same time.

Think about how long it would take you to track down all of the resources for each member of your family to connect with God on the same topic. Who has that kind of time? We do! It's not that we have nothing else to do, we are just passionate about D6. So look no further, we have created the resource for which you are looking, and it works!

D6 Devotional Magazines are full-color, interactive, fun, and exciting tools to connect with God and with each other.

Subscribe now!
800.877.7030
D6family.com

Does Christianity work in real life anymore?

If you have asked, "Where has all the integrity gone?" or "What does integrity look like in today's complex world?" this book is what you're looking for. **GARNETT REID** shares examples from **the life of Job** and shows what it means to live with integrity.

SEP 2 0 2024